Mayor

Julie Murray

Abdo
MY GOVERNMENT
Kids

abdopublishing.com

Published by Abdo Kids, a division of ABDO, PO Box 398166, Minneapolis, Minnesota 55439.
Copyright © 2018 by Abdo Consulting Group, Inc. International copyrights reserved in all countries.
No part of this book may be reproduced in any form without written permission from the publisher.

Printed in the United States of America, North Mankato, Minnesota.

102017

012018

THIS BOOK CONTAINS
RECYCLED MATERIALS

Photo Credits: AP Images, Getty Images, iStock, Shutterstock

Production Contributors: Teddy Borth, Jennie Forsberg, Grace Hansen

Design Contributors: Christina Doffing, Candice Keimig, Dorothy Toth

Publisher's Cataloging in Publication Data

Names: Murray, Julie, author.

Title: Mayor / by Julie Murray.

Description: Minneapolis, Minnesota : Abdo Kids, 2018. | Series: My government |
    Includes glossary, index and online resource (page 24).

Identifiers: LCCN 2017942864 | ISBN 9781532103988 (lib.bdg.) | ISBN 9781532105104 (ebook) |
    ISBN 9781532105661 (Read-to-me ebook)

Subjects: LCSH: Mayors--United States--Juvenile literature. | Municipal government--United States--
    Juvenile literature.

Classification: DDC 352.232160973--dc23

LC record available at https://lccn.loc.gov/2017942864

Table of Contents

Mayor. 4

What is the
Mayor's Job? 22

Glossary. 23

Index 24

Abdo Kids Code. 24

Mayor

A mayor leads a city or town.

4

The city is in charge of many things.

CITY HALL

7

The city runs the schools.

Hugo reads.

The city fixes the roads.

The city takes care of the parks.

Lucy plays with her friends.

Mayors help make laws.
Lola walks her dog on a
leash. It is a law.

They talk to people. The mayor listens to Gus.

Most mayors are **elected**. People **vote** for who they want.

Who is your mayor?

What is the Mayor's Job?

head of the city

make city laws

oversee city departments

talk and listen
to the citizens

Glossary

elected
chosen to hold public office.

law
the system of rules a country or community recognizes.

vote
a formal decision one makes (usually on a ballot) between two or more people for a job.

Index

citizens 16

election 18

laws 14

parks 12

responsibilities 4, 6, 8, 10, 12, 14, 16

roads 10

schools 8

vote 18

Abdo Kids ONLINE

FREE! ONLINE MULTIMEDIA RESOURCES

Visit **abdokids.com** and use this code to access crafts, games, videos, and more!

Abdo Kids Code:
MMK3988